ALL FEELINGS ARE OKAY

Written & Illustrated By
Emily Hayes

Scared

Grumpy

Happy

Angry

Sad

SEL

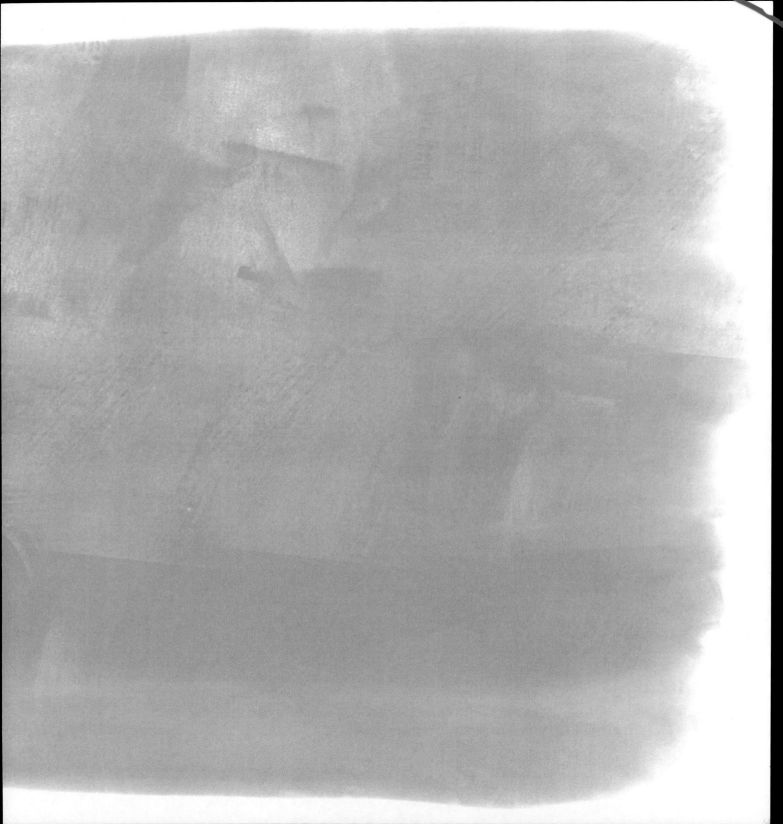

I'm so **bored** on this gloomy old afternoon,
I sure wish something would change my mood.
Oh, how I wish my friends could come over.
No, today couldn't possibly sink any lower.

Do you want to know how I felt yesterday? I was so **happy** and thought it was the best day!

I explored and went on many adventures.
I climbed lots of trees and looked for lost treasures.

I wish every day could be that way
When I could go outside with my friends and play.
But today, I am in another kind of mood.
For some reason, I have a **grumpy** attitude.

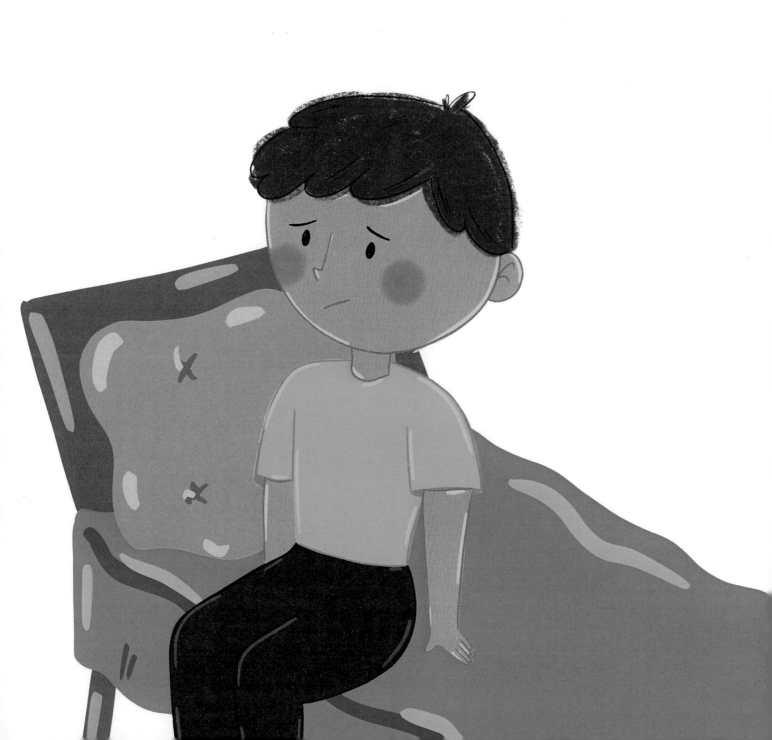

Sometimes, **happiness** comes to me just like that,
I would do anything to have that feeling back.
I'll sit and wait with anticipation.
I can pass the time with my imagination.

I feel **sad** and want to make **unhappy** faces.
I guess I'll stay home and not go any places.
My parents are too busy for me as well.
They didn't pay attention to me even when I yelled.

They're spending a lot of time in the kitchen.
I bet they're cooking dinner, and it's chicken.
Yuck. Chicken, again? Why can't we have what I want?
Something like frosted cake or a jelly-filled croissant.

Lonely

Sad

There are some days when I don't feel so sad.
On these days, I feel **frustrated** or even **mad**.
Have you ever wanted to just act out?
When you want to make **mean** faces or even shout?

Irritated

Upset

Grumpy

Frustrated

Confused

Then suddenly, I heard a loud knock on the door,
I heard thunder crashing and the rain started to pour.
I ran upstairs **scared** and hid in the attic.
Was it a monster or was I just being dramatic?

My mom and dad called me to come downstairs,
They were making me face my fears which wasn't fair!
"I'm not coming downstairs to be eaten!" I screamed.
"Trust us," my parents said. "We'll get you ice cream."

I was **nervous** but I thought, "I sure could go for some ice cream."
I trusted my parents that things wouldn't be what they seemed.
I took a big gulp, and then walked down the stairs.
I heard lots of rumbling — what was down there, a bunch of bears?

The lights turned on, and I couldn't believe my eyes.
All of my friends were here and they yelled, "SURPRISE!"
Why were they here? Did they come to cheer me up?
So this is what mom and dad had been setting up.

I don't know how I could have forgotten.
How could I have spent the day feeling so rotten?
Yesterday may have felt like it was my birthday,
But as it turns out, TODAY is my special day.

Happy

Surprised

Now I'm more **happy** than
any other day,
Sometimes it's okay for our
emotions to sway.

Disappointed

Optimistic

Furious

Grumpy

It's easy to go quickly from
happy to **sad**,
Or from **hopeful** or **nervous** to
very horribly **mad**.

Our **feelings** are what make us human and extra unique.
Even if, on a bad day, they make us feel **bleak**.
So if you're feeling **down** and you don't know what to do,
Just remember all your feelings are what make you - **YOU!**

Made in United States
North Haven, CT
03 August 2024

55702242R00020